COOL CAREERS WITHOUT COLLEGE

CAREERS FOR PEOPLE WHO LOVE
KIDS

Morgan Williams

ROSEN
PUBLISHING

New York

Published in 2021 by The Rosen Publishing Group, Inc.
29 East 21st Street, New York, NY 10010

Copyright © 2021 by The Rosen Publishing Group, Inc.

First Edition

Portions of this work were originally authored by Harriet Webster and published as *Cool Careers Without College for People Who Love to Work with Children*. All new material in this edition authored by Morgan Williams.

Library of Congress Cataloging-in-Publication Data

Names: Williams, Morgan.
Title: Careers for people who love kids / Morgan Williams.
Description: New York : Rosen Publishing, 2021. | Series: Cool careers
without college | Includes bibliographical references and index.
Identifiers: ISBN 9781499468793 (pbk.) | ISBN 9781499468809 (library bound)
Subjects: LCSH: Vocational guidance--Juvenile literature. |
Child care--Vocational guidance--Juvenile literature. | Coaching
(Athletics)--Vocational guidance--Juvenile literature.
Classification: LCC HF5381.2 W551 2021 | DDC 649'.023'73--dc23

Some of the images in this book illustrate individuals who are models. The depictions do not imply actual situations or events.

Manufactured in China

Find us on

CONTENTS

INTRODUCTION

I t takes a special person to work with children on a daily basis. Most people who do are passionate about helping the next generation learn, develop, and adapt. From day care workers to school bus drivers, the adults who interact with children have the ability to affect their lives and put them on a path toward future success.

Jobs that involve interacting with and taking care of children every day come with their own sets of advantages and challenges. The most obvious benefit to pursuing a career in this field is that you'll be getting paid to influence the next generation. The most obvious difficulty is that some kids can be rowdy and disrespectful to someone in charge—and that could be you. However, if you're interested in making working with children your career, the positives far outweigh the potential negatives of most of these jobs.

There are more job opportunities than you might think if you're interested in working with kids, and not all of them require an advanced education. You may already have experience babysitting, and moving on to full-time childcare positions will be easy. If you're an artist, you might be surprised at how eager children are to learn your skills—and how much parents are willing to pay a good enrichment instructor. Sports fanatics don't have to worry, either—youth coaching is not only alive and well, it's becoming even more popular as parents want their kids to be healthy and happy.

While you can't become a teacher without a college degree, becoming a teacher's assistant is an attractive career path for many who want to help teach kids. If you want to be involved in schools but can't see yourself in the classroom, a career as a school secretary could be just what you're looking for.

There are endless opportunities available if you're willing to work for them. As long as you have a love of children, a good work ethic, and the desire to learn, there's no doubt you'll be able to find a career that involves working with kids.

CHAPTER 1

TAKING CARE

Childcare is one of the most important businesses in the world. Many parents need to work, and few families are wealthy enough to afford a private, in-home babysitter or nanny every day. If you enjoy spending time with children, encouraging their play, sparking their creativity and learning, and think you could find satisfaction working with kids, a job in the childcare industry may be the right career move for you.

THE MANY FORMS OF CHILDCARE

Childcare workers can be employed in a wide variety of settings. Some care for children in the child's home. Others work at a day care center or in the home of another caregiver. About 25 percent of childcare workers are self-employed, taking care of children in their own homes. No matter the setting, there are few jobs more important than taking care of the needs of children while their parents are at work.

A lot of teenagers get great childcare experience by babysitting on evenings or weekends.

If you've ever earned extra money working as a babysitter, you've already experienced a job as a childcare worker. Your primary responsibility in this role is keeping the child (or children) safe and happy in your care. As a childcare worker, you'll spend much of your day taking care of children's basic needs, which may include preparing and serving nutritious snacks and meals, helping them dress, helping them stay clean and healthy, and making sure they get enough rest.

Some childcare workers specialize in infant care. They're familiar with a baby's needs and know how to comfort an infant who is distressed. These specialist workers must also have enormous patience and the ability to stay calm under stress. When an infant won't nap or cries for long periods of time, infant care providers must stay composed. They prepare bottles and change diapers. They know how to hold a baby properly, and they're knowledgeable about which positions an infant should sleep in. Most of all, the best childcare workers in infant care are those who truly enjoy tending to babies.

TAKING ON AN IMPORTANT ROLE

It's very important that childcare workers enjoy children and take pleasure in caring for them. Because of the long periods of time they spend with children every day, they have a significant effect on the children's development. A good childcare worker recognizes that part of their job is to encourage children's intellectual, social, and emotional development. Instead of sitting children in front of a TV for extended periods, a good childcare worker plays games with them, reads books to them, takes them out for walks, initiates arts and crafts projects, and helps them master basic skills, such as zipping up a jacket or catching a ball. Childcare workers who are responsible for more than one child also need to teach children how to get along with others,

Taking care of children—especially in groups—is more than just fun and games. You'll also teach them valuable life lessons.

and they need to understand how to settle conflicts between children as well.

A competent caregiver respects the value of play in children's lives. They know that building with blocks and completing puzzles are ways to introduce a child to basic math and problem-solving concepts. Similarly, making up stories, playing dress up, or producing an elaborate tea party, complete with stuffed animal guests, are all ways to stimulate language and social growth.

Another important part of a childcare worker's job is to communicate regularly and effectively with the child's parents. Parents need to hear about any problems that crop up while the child is in day care. They need to be informed about the child's accomplishments and fears, as well as any behavioral issues that arise. If you work in a day care center, there will probably be a set of rules or guidelines that specify how to communicate with parents. For example, the center may send a notebook home with the child each day, in which the childcare worker notes any particular problems or developments in the child's daily life. The parents may be encouraged to write back with their comments, concerns, or questions. At other centers, parents and caretakers sit down together at regular intervals, likely weekly or monthly, to discuss the child and their development.

While the majority of childcare workers take care of children who are five years old or younger, there are also positions in which children need supervision in before- or after-school programs. Childcare workers in these positions take care of elementary school–age kids between the time parents leave for work and school starts or between the time school lets out and the parents return home from work. Some caregivers mix full-time care of preschoolers with the before- and after-school care of older children. Others choose to work part-time and provide only before- and after-school care. Some of these part-timers become full-time caregivers during school vacation periods, offering working parents a safe, fun place where they can leave their children while they're at work.

WHAT YOU NEED

Education and training requirements for childcare workers are different from one state to another. Each state has unique requirements for anyone who wants to become a licensed childcare provider. In general, most childcare workers with high school diplomas can qualify for a position. Corporate day care centers and government-funded programs often have more difficult barriers to entry. These positions may require a childcare worker to have at least an associate's, or two-year, degree in early childhood education. For many local positions, however, a high school education should be sufficient.

JOB OUTLOOK

While compensation for childcare workers is generally on the low end, additional education can create a pathway to higher wages. Some day care centers offer benefits, such as health insurance and retirement plans. The majority of childcare workers, though, do not receive much in the way of benefits.

Both part-time and full-time jobs in childcare are widely available, and there are many opportunities to get in the field. Because the pay is relatively low, the industry experiences a lot of turnover in employees.

According to the U.S. government's Bureau of Labor Statistics, there were more than 1 million childcare jobs across the country in 2018. The number of available childcare jobs is expected to slowly increase between 2018 and 2028.

Even though job growth is relatively slow in this field, there will always be a demand for skilled childcare workers—after all, parents will always need to work, and their children will need to be supervised. Overall, there are likely to be many openings in this field if you want to join the industry.

CHAPTER 2

YOUTH COACHING

Millions of adults across the United States grew up playing youth sports, whether through their school or as part of a community league. Recognizing how important physical activity is, many parents enroll their children in sports organizations from a young age. With so many youngsters on the playing field, it's only natural that there is a need for qualified youth coaches to get them ready, teach them both athletic and life skills, and continue the country's great sporting traditions.

SPORTS FOR ALL AGES

Sports have been a major part of U.S. society for a long time. More recently, there have been movements—supported by both the government and activists—to encourage fitness as part of general health. As a result, organized youth sports have expanded greatly in recent years. Parents want their children to grow up active, and they want them to

As parents encourage their kids to develop healthy habits, youth sports participation will continue to increase.

be well supervised as they get (or stay) in shape. Participation in organized soccer and baseball leagues begins as young as six years of age, and many kids try out for competitive teams before age ten. Along with increased participation from parents and children comes greater opportunity for an aspiring youth coach.

Youth athletic teams are often coached by parents who want to be involved with their kid's activities— but who may not be particularly passionate or knowledgeable about that sport. Parent coaches often welcome assistance from a teenager who plays the sport, knows the rules inside out, and is familiar with practice drills that can help younger kids master the skills of the game. Offering to help out is an excellent way to get a taste of what coaching is like. It also provides you with practical experience you can list on your résumé when you apply for a paying job in a youth sports program.

While most coaching jobs are primarily about managing a team and utilizing players in the most effective way—with the goal of winning games—coaching a group of children is more about being a good teacher and a positive role model than striving for victory at all times. Through sports, children acquire new skills. They develop their gross motor (large muscle) skills, and they also learn about socializing through their interaction with other players. In addition, they often become more fit and develop confidence and positive self-esteem.

There are specific skills that all sports require, and as a youth coach, you must be able to demonstrate those skills to kids. In addition, while training, you'll need to direct and correct young players without resorting to criticism that will discourage them. Patience, a sense of humor, and a positive, upbeat attitude are key components of being an effective coach when it comes to working with children. You will need to figure out how to manage practice sessions and games so that weaker players have the opportunity to improve and gain experience alongside the stronger players. You also need to be prepared to deal with difficult personal situations. For example, a group of kids may make fun of a teammate, or parents may criticize your coaching style and second-guess your decisions. You'll need to learn how to cope with these situations and more.

Working with older children—including teenagers—involves many of the same potential challenges and requires many of the same qualities as working with younger children. In addition, these positions involve setting limits and imposing consequences for any player who breaks the rules or behaves inappropriately—no matter how valuable they might be to the team. A superstar player who is caught smoking, for example, should be penalized the same as an average player who is doing the same. Preteens and teens are sometimes eager to push limits and see what they can get away with.

If you are willing and able to apply rules evenly, learn the details of regulations, and make quick decisions under pressure, you may want to try serving as a referee or official. In addition to the capacity to make fast, fair calls under stress, officiating youth sports requires the ability to remain calm and clearheaded in the face of criticism and heckling, which can come from players, coaches, and spectators—especially parents. Like coaches, people who umpire youth sports need to always remember that their primary role is to make certain that the players have a positive experience. Your responsibilities should never be affected by the behavior of parents who care more about the outcome of a competition than the well-being of the players.

ON-FIELD CREDENTIALS

The type and amount of education and training required of coaches and referees varies based on the specific sport and the level of play. Elementary and secondary schools often ask their own teachers

When you're just starting out, look for opportunities to assist more experienced coaches.

to fill coaching slots before hiring outside candidates. One of the most common ways to secure an entry-level part-time position—such as an assistant coaching job—is to volunteer to work with the paid coach. You can also get on-the-job experience by volunteering to coach or officiate for intramural or community leagues.

There are countless organized youth sports out there, and, as such, there are many organizations that offer certification courses that indicate you've achieved a particular level of expertise. Most certification programs require participation in a camp, clinic, or school setting, in addition to some online components.

WHAT TO EXPECT

Compensation for those employed in youth sports will vary tremendously depending on your education and certification. Many of the coaches who work in community sports leagues with young children are unpaid. Those who coach teens often work part-time and are paid on an hourly or per-event basis. Salaried positions are available, typically through schools or large amateur leagues, and they generally offer superior pay. However, many salaried coaching positions are reserved for those with advanced education or years of experience.

Though most people associate youth coaching with schools, only 18 percent of 2018's coaches in the United States were employed by schools. As amateur and youth sports leagues have continued to spread, opportunities have increased for self-employed workers in the field. In 2018, an estimated 11 percent of coaches were self-employed, offering their skills on a freelance basis. Though freelancing can be risky, it can also be a great opportunity to gain experience or just make some extra money on weekends.

Jobs in this area are expected to increase very quickly between 2018 and 2028, with a projected 11 percent growth. Opportunities for those who want to work with young people are most often available to people interested in part-time coaching and officiating jobs at the high school level.

CHAPTER 3

THE CROWD-PLEASER

One of the most popular industries in the world is the entertainment business. From dancers to singers to actors to musicians, there are countless jobs and gigs available for those with an artistic talent. However, instead of trying to reach Hollywood or sign a record deal, you should carefully consider the benefits of kick-starting your performance career as a children's entertainer. Working events such as children's birthday parties, you can build up a solid portfolio of your artistic skills—and you'll get to spend time making kids smile to boot.

SINGING AND DANCING AND MORE

If you've developed your talent as a singer, dancer, actor, or other type of entertainer—and you believe you'd enjoy performing in front of children—you should consider turning your hobby into a career.

As a children's entertainer, you may find yourself performing in schools, youth centers, hospitals, day care centers, and summer camps, as well as at festivals and birthday parties.

Many people who work to entertain children write their own material, including original stories, songs, and routines. Some occasions, however, may call for someone to perform adaptations of old favorites. In many cases, people hire an entertainer for their kids because their material conveys a message appropriate to the age of the audience. The most successful performers are those who are in tune with the needs and interests of their young audience members.

To succeed in this field, you need to understand and enjoy spending time with children. That means recognizing that young audiences will want to sit still only for short periods of time. That is why many established performers structure their routines so that there are opportunities for children to become involved. For example, a folk singer might encourage children to sing along or to act out a song with body motions; while a musician performing traditional African music might urge audience members to stomp their feet or clap their hands to mark the rhythm. A clown or magician might ask for volunteers who can participate in tricks.

Children's performers work either independently or as part of a troupe, or a collection of other entertainers. Many do both, serving in troupes most of the time and freelancing to earn extra cash occa-

A big part of making children happy is getting them involved with your performances.

sionally. As an independent performer, you will need to be a capable businessperson as well as an artist. Independent artists of all kinds need to publicize

their acts to get jobs. You'll need to make up a contract for each job that states the agreed-upon fee; the date, time, and length of the performance; and any other important details. You'll also be responsible for making and transporting the necessary costumes, makeup, and props or scenery for each of your performances.

Most children's performers walk this career path because they have been happily involved in the arts for a long time—often from when they were young children themselves. If you find yourself attracted to a career in this industry, it's a good idea to participate in as many kinds of arts-related experiences as you can. This includes going outside your comfort zone to become more well-rounded. For example, dancers should explore theater, actors should dabble in music, and clowns should explore dancing. The reason for this is simple: the more versatile you are as a performer, the more likely it is that you can create an act that works with a variety of audiences. Similarly, relying on your major instrument (such as guitar) but also working several other instruments (such as harmonicas or drums) into your act will provide the kind of variety that can hold a child's attention. If you're a puppeteer, preparing a show appropriate for preschoolers and another production geared to six- to nine-year-olds will improve your opportunity to find work.

Earning a living as any kind of performer is not easy, especially if you're aiming to entertain children. Part-time schedules are common, and you'll likely need to work frequently on weekends and holidays. You can also expect up and down periods in your employment. It is particularly difficult to get a regular schedule of gigs (appearances) when you're just starting out. For this reason, many performers supplement their earnings with traditional part-time jobs that are completely unrelated to their work in the performing arts.

Some aspiring performers try out to work for theme parks that feature children's characters, typically dressed in costumes. Many of these parks, from local attractions to big-name corporations, hire talented teenagers with experience in the performing arts. You might find yourself parading through

Clowns have been making kids smile and laugh for centuries. You can get experience in entertainment by volunteering as one.

the park, dressed up in an over-the-top outfit and participating in song-and-dance routines with your coworkers. Working at a job like this is good experience, giving you a feel for how young audiences react and helping you to figure out how to best use your talents and personality to keep kids interested.

GETTING READY

Although no formal or advanced education is required to become a children's entertainer, experience and flexibility are key. The more you know about your craft, the more likely you'll be to succeed in this extremely competitive industry. Take classes and lessons to strengthen your artistic skills and develop new ones. Sign up for interactive workshops taught by experienced performers. Participate in high school and community productions when they're available, and try to accept technical assignments, such as helping with costumes or working the lights, in addition to onstage opportunities. The idea is to get as much practice as you can in front of a live audience. These experiences will also help you network with people in the field who may be able to help you to land jobs.

You can also get experience by volunteering to entertain at a young family member's birthday party or at a day care center or hospital. Start to experiment with writing your own songs or skits. Read a lot of children's literature. Also be sure to attend performances by a broad variety of children's entertainers so you can get a sense of what works and what doesn't from someone already established in the industry.

TOUGH SHOW BUSINESS

Full-time salaried positions are extremely rare in this field. Many performers are paid by the appearance, and earnings are relatively low in general because of the downtime between different gigs. Entertainers are often waiting—and hoping—to get their "big break," which can come in the form of a high-profile gig, a popular song, or simply by getting the attention of a talent agent.

Though it can be difficult to break into show business, there is always a demand for entertainment. Though work for entertainers is not expected to grow substantially from 2018 to 2028, there are always opportunities to be found for someone with passion, talent, and a good work ethic. Parents are eager to expose their children to the arts. The rise of online entertainment opportunities may also increase the amount of work available for children's entertainers who can produce their own content. Although the competition is challenging, the field experiences a lot of turnover as performers get tired of the irregular hours and modest wages, eventually moving on to other careers.

CHAPTER 4

DAY CARE DREAMS

Many people dream of coming up with a great idea for a unique business, making and implementing a plan to start it, and striking it rich. However, you don't have to reinvent the wheel to become a successful business owner, especially if you want to start a family day care center. Though some day care providers work at a childcare center as employees, many are entrepreneurs. Day care is a great industry to achieve an ambition to be your own boss, though there are many challenges and hazards that come along with it.

GETTING STARTED

Because taking care of children is such an important job, nearly all cities and states have unique licensing requirements that must be met before someone can begin work. The first step for anyone who wants to work at a day care is to meet these requirements and get officially certified. You may need to take classes and pass a background check to prove that you're qualified to take care of children. If you're starting your own day care business, you'll need to make sure the space you use—whether it's your own home or a rented building—has also been approved for children.

Another component of operating your own day care is keeping track of expenses and revenue. You'll need to determine how much to charge clients, and you'll have to use an accounting system to keep track of your money. There are many responsibilities that

Keeping detailed business records is the first step to success if you want your day care to succeed.

come with running your own business. These include maintaining and cleaning your space, purchasing supplies and equipment, filing the appropriate business-related forms, and keeping records for each child (health forms, permission slips, and so on). Be ready to advertise your business and interview with parents who are interested in your services. In addition, it's important to communicate regularly with the parents of the children in your care.

Whether you're operating a day care or simply working at one, the most important part of your job is to provide each child with a safe, stimulating, and happy experience. Parents want their children to be active and learning while they're at day care, not sitting in front of a TV or playing with a tablet all day. Occupying children in a meaningful way for hours each day is tough, and it requires lots of advance planning.

Skilled caregivers prepare a daily schedule of activities that includes both quiet and active times, as well as opportunities for both individual and group activities. If you are caring for children of different ages, you will need to organize different projects for each age group. The more you know about child development—such as what kinds of activities will be helpful and fun for different ages—the better you will be able to engage children in projects that are interesting.

Children learn best through play. By giving children access to dress-up clothes, puppets, dolls, blocks, pots and pans, and other materials that encourage them to use their imaginations, you're giving them the opportunity to grow and learn. Creative and expressive activities like dancing, singing, painting, and acting help children develop their language skills and build self-esteem. Taking walks in the woods or visiting nearby playgrounds—with parents' approval—are other types of activities to build into a day care schedule.

Another important part of day care work is understanding child-staff ratios. Parents and government agencies both pay a lot of attention to these numbers, which compare the number of children to the number of caretakers in a day care. For example, childcare experts recommend that there is one caretaker for every three or four infants (under 15 months); one for every three to four toddlers (12 to 28 months); and one for every four to six children (2 to 3 years).

Working as a family day care provider can be physically tiring. Caring for infants and toddlers involves a lot of standing, stooping, and lifting. Keeping up with energetic preschoolers and keeping them safe requires constant mental attention and a quick response time in case something goes wrong.

There are many positives to working in day care. The most important, of course, is being able to spend your entire workday with children. If you aren't passionate about doing that, this is not the career for you. If you're running a day care out of your own home, you won't need to travel to work. Owning your own business, in general, comes with its own perks, like being your own boss and setting

A strong desire to work with children every day is the main reason many are in this field.

your own work schedule and hours. As a day care operator, however, you'll have to be highly attentive to laws and regulations, and if you're working out of your own home, you'll be giving up a lot of privacy, as you let children and their parents in every day.

GETTING LICENSED

Each state has its own regulations and requirements for obtaining a license to provide day care, but one common qualification is to have at least a high school diploma. If you want to be a self-employed family day care provider, the more experience and training you have, the more successful you will be—and the more you can charge for your services.

To prepare yourself for this career, it may be worthwhile to find classes—online or at a local community center or college—in early childhood development, first aid, nutrition, and the arts. If you want to advance in the business, you may want to consider getting an associate's degree in early childhood education in the future. There is also a widely recognized program offered by the Council for Professional Recognition that awards candidates with a Child Development Associate certification. This qualification is not only highly recommended for anyone working in childcare, it is also sometimes a requirement for state licensing.

GETTING PAID

Like in most fields, the more education, experience, and training you have as a day care provider, the more money you can make. If you're a self-employed family day care operator, you won't make a salary in the traditional sense. Instead, your earnings will vary according to how many hours you work and the ages and number of children you care for. People typically pay more for care of infants, therefore those workers earn more than those taking care of children of other ages.

Just as with all childcare workers, day care workers and owners will have solid employment opportunities in the future. Though some parents are giving up work to stay at home with their children, many are unable to do so—and they need somewhere for their children to go when they head to work. All parents are concerned with the welfare of their children, and day care providers should offer personal service that makes everyone happy.

CHAPTER 3

HELPING THOSE IN NEED

Have you ever wanted to make a difference in the world, especially in the lives of struggling children and families? A job as a human service assistant may be for you. People in this position are responsible for working with a wide variety of kids in need, from those with physical or mental disabilities to those who are going through emotional hardships. If you become a human service assistant, you may also become involved in preventive outreach work, which means trying to help kids who may be headed down a hazardous path. No matter what role you fill in this career, you'll be lending a helping hand to those who need it most.

A CAREER OF SERVICE

In most fields, the word "client" refers to a customer or someone who is paying you for a good or service. In the world of human services, however, the word "client" refers to the person who is receiving services

Some jobs in human services involve a lot of one-on-one time with kids.

or care. Human service assistants provide their clients with both indirect and direct services. Indirect services are tasks that don't involve spending actual time with the client. These tasks often include sorting through paperwork, such as figuring out whether a child is eligible to receive a particular benefit. For example, if you work in a public welfare agency,

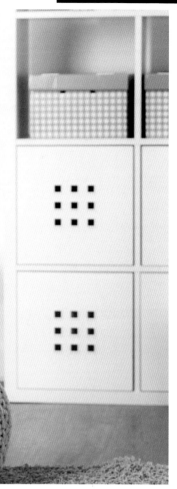

you might examine a parent's tax documents and related information to determine if a child qualifies for publicly supported health benefits.

Direct services are tasks that involve actual contact with the client. Imagine that you work in a community center. Presenting the children at the center with different options for how they spend their after-school time—and helping them decide which program they would like to join—is an example of a direct service. These kinds of tasks, and others, will be a big part of this job.

As a human service worker employed by a community center or government agency, an important part of your job will likely be to provide your clients with a safe, constructive environment where they can discuss their concerns and explore healthy social and recreational activities. If you work for a shelter, your responsibilities may include caring for children while their parents participate in counseling or job-training programs. As an employee at a residential facility, you might instruct intellectually or physically disabled children in independent living skills, such as bathing and dressing themselves.

Human service assistants work with young people in a variety of settings, including residential facilities, such as group homes or shelters. This career path may also lead you to working in clinics, mental health centers, community centers, day treatment programs, and psychiatric hospitals. Many of these positions ask you to work a 40-hour week and often spend time on the road, visiting clients and their families at home. About 20 percent of human service employees work for state and local governments. Most government positions are with public welfare agencies or at facilities for clients who are intellectually, developmentally, or physically disabled.

Human service assistants often work closely with other professionals with similar jobs, such as social workers, psychologists, and psychiatrists. They help their clients participate in treatment plans designed by the professional staff, providing emotional support and encouragement. Many human service employees are also responsible for instructing clients in areas such as effective communication or appropriate behavior.

As a human service assistant, you'll serve as an important link between a child and their family, communicating the child's needs, progress, and problems with whatever program they're in. You'll also read about each child's specific situation and gain insight on how to improve their life. Many workers report that the job is satisfying and gives a feeling of having made a difference in a child's life. At the same time, however, the work can be emotionally draining, leading to a high turnover rate in this field.

To succeed in human services, you'll need to be able to communicate with others.

Workers who take advantage of on-the-job training and other educational opportunities are rewarded with increased responsibilities and better pay.

BEFORE YOU SERVE

While some employers require only that human service workers have a high school diploma, most prefer applicants with some post–high school education. This often means acquiring at least an associate's degree, but it is also possible to start in this field with just a certificate, which would not require attending college. Community colleges often offer certification programs, where students learn basic skills, such as how to record data and conduct client interviews. Students may also practice problem-solving techniques and become familiar with crisis intervention procedures. Employers look positively on high school graduates with on-the-job experience, such as working or volunteering at summer camps or recreational programs for disabled children.

Because they have an important and difficult job, most employers offer their human service assistants frequent continuing training opportunities. Employees with no education beyond high school are also likely to receive extensive hands-on training at the start of their employment.

This job is expected to experience extremely fast growth from 2018 to 2028, with an estimated 52,200 jobs added to the field in that time span. As the number of career opportunities increases, so too does competition. Many skilled youths will likely be applying to the same jobs as you, so it's important to get as much experience, training, and education as you can before trying to break into the industry. Once you're in, however, you can expect to receive generous compensation, good job security, and—most importantly—a sense of fulfillment every day as you work with children in need.

CHAPTER 6

BEING BOOKISH

Though physical libraries may seem out of date with the rise of e-books and other digital delivery platforms, nothing could be further from the truth. Some of the main "clients" of the modern library are children, whose passion for reading is just starting to heat up. As a librarian or library assistant, you'll be directly contributing to the intellectual and creative development of kids, serving a wide variety of age ranges, from kindergarten to high school. In addition to simply checking out and reshelving books, you'll likely be responsible for putting together library programs, organizing book drives, and getting kids—and their parents—to keep coming back to their local library.

CHECKING OUT

The best part of working as a librarian or library assistant specializing in children's books is, of course, getting to interact with and inspire young

In an increasingly digital world, children's librarians are needed to help kids discover the magic of reading.

readers every time they visit. Working directly with children, you may be tasked with running a story hour, organizing a holiday crafts session, or helping kids learn to use computers to find the books they want to read. Other responsibilities include setting up informational displays and bulletin boards or helping kids settle in at listening stations where they can hear music or a recorded story. You can also help children with homework assignments that require research. Library assistants who work in school libraries also help teachers locate the materials they need.

If you want to become a library assistant, you'll likely have to accept responsibility for doing a lot of clerical chores. Typical daily tasks include checking out books for young guests, collecting overdue fines, processing new books before they're put on the shelves, reshelving returned books, and organizing magazines, pamphlets, and other materials. Library assistants also help to set up special events, such as puppet shows and programs involving visiting authors and illustrators.

Library assistants who work in school libraries most often work a standard Monday-to-Friday schedule and have the same vacations as teachers. Those who work in public libraries work on a year-round schedule and are often required to work some weekends and evenings.

Some library assistants serve as bookmobile drivers. A bookmobile is a large truck or van that has been stocked with books, which drives around to patrons who may have difficulty getting to the library. Typical destinations for these traveling libraries include neighborhoods with many elderly individuals; rural community centers; and hospitals. Bookmobiles will also stop at isolated rural schools (especially if they don't have their own libraries), day care centers, and other locations that see a lot of children, such as Boys and Girls Clubs.

EARNING A MEDAL

The Newbery Medal is the most important award given in children's literature. Named after John Newbery, an 18th-century bookseller, it was the first children's book prize in the world. Since 1922, it has been awarded to the author of the most creative and distinguished children's book of the year. How many of these medal winners have you read?

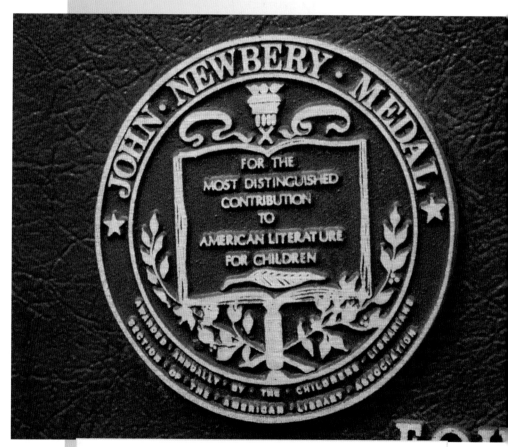

Books that are awarded the Newbery Medal are sure to become hits with kids at their school or public library.

- *The Voyages of Doctor Dolittle* by Hugh Lofting (1923)
- *A Wrinkle in Time* by Madeleine L'Engle (1963)
- *Roll of Thunder, Hear My Cry* by Mildred D. Taylor (1977)
- *Number the Stars* by Lois Lowry (1990)
- *Holes* by Louis Sachar (1999)
- *The Crossover* by Kwame Alexander (2015)
- *Merci Suárez Changes Gears* by Meg Medina (2019)

EDUCATING YOURSELF

Training, education, and experience requirements for library assistants can vary widely. Some employers require only a high school education, while others insist on some form of college degree. Strong computer skills will also help you to land a job, as will experience working with children in summer camps or after-school programs. Of course, a proven passion for books is also a must.

If you're interested in this field, a good way to gain experience to add to your résumé is to volunteer in your high school library or—even better—explore volunteer opportunities at the children's section of your local public library. Of course, any volunteering or internship opportunity at a library on weekends while you are still in school will help you gain experience and develop the skills necessary to do the job full-time. It's also wise to familiarize yourself with popular children's books, from all-time greats like *Madeline* to modern classics like the *Harry Potter* series.

Some community colleges and private two-year colleges offer an associate of arts degree in library technology. Though taking courses toward earning this degree will certainly be helpful, going to college isn't necessary. Library associations sometimes offer workshops and in-service training focusing on new developments in library operations. There are many paths to take if you want to strengthen your application for a library job.

WHAT TO LOOK FOR

Though they perform a valuable role in society, librarians and library assistants don't receive a lot of compensation. Starting salaries are relatively low, especially as an assistant, but many libraries will offer loyal and talented employees opportunities to advance, learn more, and earn more.

Because technology, including digital books, advanced a great deal in the 2010s, some public libraries across the United States closed. The Bureau of Labor Statistics reports that the overall number of library assistant positions is expected to shrink between 2018 and 2028, but don't worry. There will always be a need for librarians, especially in schools. Many communities across the country still depend on their local libraries for entertainment and education.

CHAPTER 7

TEACHING THE ARTS

O ne of the most impactful things a parent can do is introduce their children to the arts and other enrichment activities from a young age. If you're passionate about the arts, you were probably exposed as a youngster yourself! However, as many public schools slash budgets and cut arts programs, more and more parents are looking to private tutors, called enrichment teachers, to get their kids involved in music, visual arts, and more. If you have an artistic streak in you and you'd like to pass that down to the next generation, this is the career you've been waiting for.

SPECIALIZING IN ARTISTRY

Becoming a private enrichment teacher can be difficult. In addition to a passion for children and a love of teaching, you must be accomplished in the area you plan to teach. Whether you want to offer lessons in piano, violin, ballet, tap dancing, painting,

It's one thing to be a talented artist—and another to be able to teach those skills.

ceramics, or any other art form, you need to feel very confident in your ability. You must also be good at teaching—which requires a whole different set of skills from those related to being an artist. No matter how gracefully you dance, you won't succeed as a dance teacher unless you can excite your young students about what they're about to learn!

Good teachers give lessons in a variety of forms. Not only does this keep their pupils interested, but it also helps because different children learn in different ways. The ability to explain an idea or procedure, demonstrate a skill, and break a challenge down into small, manageable steps is all part of being a good instructor. So, too, is the ability to make the lesson fun.

It is important to recognize that your young students will have a whole range of attitudes toward participating in your lessons. Imagine you're a piano teacher starting out with a class of three seven-year-old students. The first may be tremendously eager to take her lessons. The second may be taking lessons only because his parents think it would help him. The third may have enrolled because her best friend is taking lessons elsewhere and she doesn't want to be left behind. Because you must teach all three equally, you need to accept each child's motivations and recognize that many children are sampling a variety of enrichment activities before finding one that they really enjoy. Don't take it personally if a student doesn't enjoy your lessons.

If you're a teacher of the arts, you can expect to see each child about once a week. Music teachers most often give private lessons, while dance and art teachers often give lessons to small groups. Each session—no matter the form—must be carefully planned with clear objectives and a variety of activities.

Before, during, and after your lessons, it's important to listen attentively to your students. The pleasure a child gets out of an enrichment activity is closely related to the quality of the relationship they have with their teacher. The more you encourage and support your students, the harder they'll work to master the skills you're teaching—and the more they'll enjoy their lessons with you. At the same time, a good teacher doesn't focus on their pupils' mistakes, instead pushing young students to experiment and explore as they discover their own creative spark.

Most parents are realistic enough to realize that their child is not likely to turn out to be a superstar artist. Instead, they recognize that enrichment lessons have lots of advantages, regardless of whether or not their child becomes a master. Through their participation, children will develop hand-eye coordination, physical strength, the ability to concentrate, a sense of discipline, and a sense of their strengths. They're also likely to develop an appreciation for the arts and a lifelong hobby that gives them pleasure long after they leave your class. In some cases, they may be inspired by your teaching and even grow up to become professionals.

GETTING SOME EXPERIENCE

As with any job, the more experience you have as an enrichment teacher, the better. Here are some ways you can get started:

- Ask a parent in your neighborhood if you can give their child lessons free of charge.
- Ask an established art or dance teacher if you can assist with group lessons.
- Offer to give group lessons to a local scout troop.
- Volunteer to teach at an after-school program.
- Get a summer job as a camp counselor where you can offer instruction in your specialty as one of the camp's activities.

Summer camps offer children of all ages the chance to learn new skills—and you could be the one to teach them about art.

Enrichment teachers who concentrate on younger children, around preschool age, frequently offer morning classes. Those who focus on older children, in middle and high school, typically work around school hours, scheduling lessons in the late afternoon, on weekends, and sometimes in the evening.

TRAINING FOR TEACHING

The most important skill an art teacher needs is a strong background in the subject they want to teach. Many teachers are students of the arts themselves. In other words, they continue to take lessons or do research to improve their own skills. If you do take lessons when you're not teaching, look to your teacher for valuable advice as you begin to deal with your own pupils.

Before you try to strike out professionally, you can look for volunteer opportunities at local school districts. Some areas offer summer programs for younger students, such as putting on a play. Even if acting isn't your talent, programs like this still need people to teach students about singing, making costumes, and painting sets. You may even learn a thing or two yourself.

In addition to your enrichment activity of choice—whether it's visual, written, or performance art—you should have a working knowledge of the broader artistic field. If you specialize in piano, for example, you should also try to learn several other instruments. Similarly, a ballet instructor should be familiar with other styles of dance, such as jazz, tap, ballroom, and hip-hop. A painter who teaches children's art classes should know how to work with clay and photography as well. Learning multiple artistic skills will help you teach your own specialty even better.

While some enrichment teachers are employed by private organizations and after-school programs, most are self-employed. Being self-employed in this field means advertising yourself, connecting with

Becoming a freelance instructor will give you the ability to pick your own clients and set your own prices.

parents, and leading as many classes as possible to make ends meet. If you become a freelance art teacher, you'll likely charge an hourly rate, which you can increase as you develop experience, a reputation, and a strong client base. That rate typically ranges from $20 to $60 per hour for private instruction. Instructors who teach classes usually charge less per pupil, but may make slightly more for the entire class.

The future is bright for aspiring private enrichment teachers. Across the United States, many public schools are reducing funding to arts programs. This means parents will look elsewhere if they want to get their kids involved in music, painting, or dancing. Even in school districts that have a strongly supported arts curriculum, students are often encouraged to take private lessons after school or on weekends to improve their skills. Overall, if you want to try teaching arts as your career, you should feel confident testing the market.

CHAPTER 8

NANNIES AND OTHER CAREGIVERS

Historically, a woman who was employed to look after and care for children was called a nanny. Her responsibilities would include supervising play, cleaning up after the children, and other general caretaking tasks. In more modern times, nannies still exist—but today the term is used for people of all genders who provide care for children in the family's home. Sometimes the term "manny" is used for men who provide this service.

Nannies are still an important part of life for many people, typically parents who are wealthy and willing to pay a premium to have their children personally supervised in their own homes.

A DIFFERENT KIND OF CARE

Unlike most childcare and day care workers, nannies care for children in their clients' homes. Unlike babysitters, who are typically employed only for a few hours at a time, nannies spend prolonged periods of time—generally entire days, weeks, or months—with the same family. Some nannies "live in," meaning that they have a room and a bathroom (sometimes shared with the children) right in their employer's home. Others "live out" and come to work each day for a set period of time, typically leaving when one or both parents get home from work.

If you enjoy working with children, are respectful, have a sense of humor, and use common sense, you already have some of the qualifications required to be a nanny. As with all caretakers of children, a nanny needs to be able to communicate clearly with both children and parents. It is very important to understand that children have different needs at different ages. A client may have an infant and a five-year-old, and you must be able to balance taking care of both children, despite their very different needs. If you have all these attributes and are also organized and respond well in an emergency, this might be a good career choice for you.

Working as a nanny is highly demanding. If you're a live-in nanny, you may be on duty for long periods. You'll also have to adjust to living in someone else's home, and you will be giving up some of your privacy. You will be responsible for your employer's children, caring for them when they're sick, getting them to their play dates and other activities on time, preparing their meals, doing their laundry, making certain they get their homework done, disciplining them when necessary, and offering comfort and companionship. Though you may be tasked with cleaning up messes a child makes, you should not, generally, be asked to do much housework; that's not your job.

Most families in search of a nanny are looking for two things: a person with a proven passion for childcare and a person who's a good match for their children and lifestyle. They want to hire someone who is comfortable with children in the age range of their kids (taking care of an infant is very different from taking care of a six-year-old, and taking care of both at once is even tougher). Clients want to find

Nannies spend a lot of time with a single family, which helps them provide personalized care for the children.

someone who fits in with their family because a nanny will, over time, become a part of the family. They also want to find someone who will make a commitment to stay for a set period of time, typically up to a year, maybe longer.

As a potential nanny, you should be looking for the right match too. The key to finding a good position is to ask lots of questions and to take the time to get to know both the parents and the children before making a commitment. You also need to make sure you're comfortable with everything they ask you to do. If you don't think you can handle the responsibility, don't be afraid to share your concern before accepting an opportunity. It's better to find a different job than do a bad job, which could hurt your reputation.

Once you have found a position, start communicating with your clients clearly and consistently. This will be absolutely essential, helping

If you're a nanny, you'll be working with the same parents for a long time. You'll all need to be able to communicate effectively to have a good partnership.

you avoid misunderstandings and the problems that can develop from them. Since the duties of a nanny vary greatly from one job to another, it's best to have a written agreement with your employer describing your responsibilities and privileges. If you're ever asked to do something outside of that agreement,

GETTING DEFINITION

There are a lot of names for people who take care of children in their parents' homes. Though the duties they perform are similar, there are distinct differences between these positions:

Governess

A well-educated person with a solid childcare background who provides academic instruction in the home. A governess typically doesn't care for infants or do housework.

Nanny

A person who's employed by a family to take care of one or more children in their home. Responsibilities are limited to childcare and household tasks that are directly related to the children, like preparing their snacks, doing their laundry, and helping them clean their rooms.

Mother's Helper

A person who provides full-time childcare and household help for families in which one parent is usually home. A mother's helper often cares for one child while the mother attends to another child. They are sometimes left alone with the children for short periods of time.

Au Pair

Someone who lives with a family and helps out with childcare and light housework. Au pairs commonly seek placement in a foreign country (an American teenager going to France or a French teen coming to the United States, for example). They're given the opportunity to experience life in a different culture while making some money.

Babysitter

Babysitters care for children on an as-needed basis, often just for a few hours.

make sure you communicate with your clients about whether you're willing to do it or not.

PREPARING YOURSELF

Childcare and day care workers can generally find employment with a high school diploma and little experience, but nannies are often held to a higher standard. Most families prefer to hire nannies with a lot of training and experience in caring for children. However, the reality is that—because nannies are in high demand—many new hires have little previous training or experience. This is good news for you.

High school courses in child development are a good way to lay the foundation for a career as a nanny. Extensive babysitting experience is also a plus, as is any other work you can find that involves children, such as a position as a camp counselor over the summer. If you're looking for a live-in role, families will also likely expect you to hold a driver's license and to have a good driving record, as you'll probably be responsible for driving their children.

Schools that train nannies offer courses in early childhood education, nutrition, and general childcare skills. Training organizations in the United States offer a wide variety of programs, ranging from certification training that takes a few weeks to a full bachelor's degree track. If you're having trouble finding work without advanced education, try looking for a training option that works for your schedule and budget.

Because most nannies are tasked with labor-intensive, round-the-clock responsibilities, their compensation is higher than day care workers. Live-in nannies may draw a smaller paycheck, but their room and board will be paid for, which contributes to the total compensation package. Of course, the more training and experience you have, the more you can request when negotiating an agreement or finding new clients. Many families who hire a nanny are on the wealthier side and might be willing to pay a very high price for quality childcare. However, you don't want to price yourself out of the market—make sure you do your research so you know how much your skills are worth.

As with most forms of childcare, the nanny business isn't going anywhere. In fact, it may even be growing faster than other childcare fields. In 2018, the Bureau of Labor Statistics reports that 19 percent of all childcare workers were employed by private households, compared to 25 percent who worked as freelancers.

CHAPTER 2

SELLING SMILES

Think about your favorite store as a kid. Did it sell toys, or games, or candy? Maybe it didn't specialize in kids' products at all. Whatever it was, you probably always had a smile on your face when you walked through the door, because you knew you would get to see something new and there would be an employee there to tell you all about it. Now imagine working in such a store, telling a parent and their child all about the newest craze and watching them get wide-eyed and excited just like you might have done.

ADVENTURES IN RETAIL

If you think you would enjoy selling fun new products to kids and families, you may want to look for a job in retailing. More specifically, you should look for a job at a store that specializes in the sale of kids' products. These positions are available in department stores as well as in toy stores, sporting

Parents are always shopping for their kids, and there are many stores that cater directly to customers like this.

goods stores, candy stores, and stores that primarily sell children's clothing.

The major job of a salesperson in a retail environment is to provide excellent customer service. This means getting customers interested in age-appropriate products and answering their questions. It's important to be knowledgeable about both the items you're selling and the intended audience for each particular product. For example, the more you know about early childhood development, the more successful you'll be in helping parents or grandparents choose the right toy for a child of any age.

People who enjoy working with children make good salespeople in stores that sell products for youngsters because parents often take their children along when they shop. If you are patient and pleasant, customers will feel more comfortable. This means they'll be more likely to buy something, which either earns you a commission check or helps your store stay in business. Some stores with a focus on kids' goods feature activity centers, where kids can play while their parents shop. A sales associate with experience or an interest in childcare may be assigned to supervise a play area.

Other stores will encourage salespeople to demonstrate how different products work so customers can see before they buy. In the end, whether you're selling board games, basketballs, or boots, your ability to help the customer find the product most appropriate for their child is what will determine your success in this field.

As a general rule, salespeople spend long hours on their feet and often do physical work around the store when they're not selling. These tasks can include lifting boxes, stocking shelves, and moving merchandise. The work setting is typically clean and well lit. Salespeople are expected to help keep merchandise organized and attractively displayed in addition to sweeping or mopping the floor at the end of a shift.

Working in a sales-related job involves a lot more than just helping customers. You'll also be asked to make sure the store is well stocked and ready for business.

Salespeople at retail stores must also be trustworthy enough to handle large amounts of money, which is another important aspect of the job. As a salesperson, you'll have to ring up sales on a cash register or electronic terminal and handle returns or exchanges. You may also be responsible for making deposits at the end of the day and ensuring that the contents of the register match the records of sales made and returns processed.

Many of the people who work in this industry hold part-time jobs, especially when they're just starting out. Since weekends are especially busy shopping times, salespeople need to be willing to work on Saturdays or Sundays. Employers also often require evening hours and extra hours around holidays.

GETTING AN EARLY START

Most entry-level sales jobs don't require advanced education, but many employers will be happy to see a high school diploma. Proficiency in English is often required, and some larger employers may offer language training for applicants who need assistance. Applicants who have taken high school courses in marketing, accounting, and business are likely to catch the eye of a potential employer.

If you would like to work in a store that specializes in sporting goods, your experience playing a variety of sports and your ability to make informed suggestions about the equipment related to those sports is an important part of the "education" you bring to the job. Similarly, if you are seeking a job in a toy store, a résumé that lists courses in child development is likely to score you bonus points with an employer.

Salespeople almost always receive on-the-job training. In smaller stores, the manager or an experienced employee will provide instruction on how to process cash and card sales, including how to use the cash register and point-of-sale (POS) software. You'll also need to learn how to handle returns and special orders, which can be difficult before you gain experience in retail. In larger stores, new employees commonly participate in more formal training programs that last several days. In addition to learning about customer service, store policies, and security procedures, participants may receive training related to the particular type of products they will be selling. Many retailers will require that new employees participate in an online training program, which will be supplemented with hands-on experience.

Retail employees must know how to use every part of a POS system, from sales to processing returns and refunds.

It's possible for talented salespeople to be promoted into managers or executives without a college degree, but a lot of larger retailers prefer to promote workers who have earned college degrees in marketing, merchandising, or business. Computer skills are also highly valued if you want to advance. Taking courses in these areas at a community college as you continue working can improve your opportunities for advancement.

ROUGH RETAIL

Because you don't need higher education to become a retail worker, the starting wage at an entry-level position is relatively low. However, some stores add to the base wage with a commission for good sales numbers. For example, you may receive anywhere from 1 to 3 percent of the price of any items you sell. Retailers offer commissions because they believe workers will sell more passionately if there is money on the line. If you can land a job with commission potential, remember to be careful: though selling harder can make you more money, some people don't like pushy employees.

More generally, you can expect to make slightly less money at smaller stores than at bigger retail chains. In addition, consider the other benefits that are being offered as part of your total compensation package. Many large stores will offer employees insurance or retirement plans, which can sometimes offset a lower paycheck.

RETAIL REQUIREMENTS

No matter what branch of retail you try to join, there are some qualifications employers will be looking for:

- **People skills**: Your ability to understand a customer's wants and needs and serve them enthusiastically; your ability to get along with your fellow employees.
- **Flexibility**: Your ability to adjust in a fast-paced environment; your ability to perform a wide variety of tasks during the workday.
- **Decisiveness**: Your ability to be self-motivated; your ability to make quick decisions, follow through with tasks, and accept responsibility for your results.
- **Analytical skills**: Your ability to solve problems, look at data, and predict trends; your ability to establish priorities.
- **Stamina**: Your ability to maintain professional standards throughout a long workday.

As for the future of retail, things are a little rough. With the rise of online competition, many brick-and-mortar stores are having trouble keeping prices low enough to get repeat customers. After all, who wants to drive to a store when they could shop online and get a discount? As a result, jobs in retail are expected to decline by about 2 percent between 2018 and 2028, according to the Bureau of Labor Statistics. However, physical stores will never completely go out of business, so if you can prove that you're a good retail salesperson, the sky's the limit to your success.

CHAPTER 10

DRIVING THE BUS

W hether a kid loves going to school or hates it, the bottom line is that they have to get there somehow. When students have to travel more than a certain distance to go to school or when parents have work schedules that conflict with school schedules, district-sponsored school buses roll out to ferry children safely to their place of learning. The people who drive these vehicles are more than just motorists—they're skilled operators who take pride in getting their riders from home to school, and back again, safely.

BUS BUSINESS

Many school bus drivers work about 20 hours a week, bringing children to school in the morning and home in the afternoon. Some drivers increase their earnings by accepting assignments to take children on field trips or to athletic events. These extra jobs add to the overall hours worked.

Unlike public transit bus drivers, school bus drivers are not responsible for collecting fares from their passengers. In some school districts, however, they are required to check that students have bus passes. In addition to the work that goes into operating the bus, drivers must also attend to paperwork. This usually involves completing weekly reports on the number of students transported, the number of routes completed, the miles traveled, and amount of fuel consumed.

School bus drivers perform an important service that involves a high degree of responsibility. They need to be able to block out distractions from their passengers and pay careful attention to their driving, particularly in poor weather. Extra caution is required each time the bus is stopped so children can get on and off.

Drivers must also enforce the safety standards set by their school district. This typically means

School bus drivers make sure children have a reliable way to get to and from school.

making sure students are the only people boarding the bus. To further guarantee safety, they need to be able to control the behavior of their riders. When children are disruptive or loud, they can distract a driver—which puts all the passengers in jeopardy. A good school bus driver doesn't tolerate disruptive behavior. By communicating with school and bus company officials when problems arise— and quickly addressing those problems in the moment—a skilled driver can ensure the safety of their young passengers.

All across the country, schools serve children who may have a wide variety of physical, mental, and behavioral disabilities. School bus drivers need to know how to meet the needs of these special passengers. If you decide to become a school bus driver and interview with several different employers, it would be wise to ask about what training drivers receive to help them accommodate children who have special needs.

If your local school district owns and operates its own fleet of buses, the drivers are employed by the school district. A large number of districts, however, contract with a private bus company to provide transportation for its students. In this case, the driver is an employee of the bus company, not the school. In either model, the 2010s experienced a shortage of qualified candidates for the position of bus driver. This is because the qualifications and standards drivers must meet are constantly being raised.

GETTING YOUR FOOT ON THE PEDAL

All employers in this field want to see a good driving record from their applicants, and most will require a high school diploma. In many states, a background check is required before you can be hired as a school bus driver. The reason for a background check is simple: school bus drivers are given a lot of responsibility, so schools, parents, and employers need to ensure that drivers have no history of criminal activity. Potential drivers must also face drug and alcohol testing prior to employment. Some employers will continue random testing after employment to make sure their drivers are staying clean.

To qualify as a school bus driver, you must also be in good physical condition, without any chronic diseases that could reduce your ability to consistently drive safely. Good vision is also a requirement, though you should be okay if you have an up-to-date prescription for corrective lenses. On top of all that, you must be strong enough to comfortably drive the bus, which isn't as easy as driving a car.

In terms of formal qualifications, you must hold a commercial driver's license from the state in which you plan to drive before you can get hired. Because many drivers have never driven a vehicle anywhere near as large as a school bus, employers almost always provide in-depth training. Depending on state and local regulations, you'll likely participate

Operating a school bus is more than just moving a steering wheel. Buses are large vehicles that have more functions than a car.

in a training program lasting several weeks, which will include both driving and classroom instruction. This training will get you familiar with the features of the bus you'll be driving, and you'll have the opportunity to practice driving it with an experienced driver to supervise. You will learn about safe driving practices, emergency evacuation procedures, first aid, accommodating students with special needs, appropriate driver-student interactions, and the laws and school policies that regulate the operation of school buses in the area you'll be working.

DRIVING THE FUTURE

Despite having to work only during the school year—with considerable time off—school bus drivers are generally compensated fairly well. As noted, you may be able to earn overtime or additional pay by volunteering to drive children to sporting events, field trips, and other school-related functions. Though the pay is typically good, many school bus drivers don't receive comprehensive health care or retirement benefits. This is because most bus driving jobs are offered on a part-time basis, and part-time

BUS BENEFITS

Though the design of a common school bus hasn't changed much over the years, they remain some of the safest vehicles on the road. The U.S. National Highway Traffic Safety Administration reports that children riding a school bus are 70 times more likely to arrive at their destinations safely than if they rode in a car. Additionally, bus ridership removes an estimated 17 million cars from the road across the country, helping reduce pollution. Because child safety is so important, there are 10 federally supported committees and departments in the United States that regulate school buses and drivers.

employees—in any industry—are rarely given a full set of benefits. However, if you can find a job working directly for a school district, you may have a better opportunity to receive compensation beyond your paychecks. It's always helpful to compare potential employers in your area to see who can give you the best offer.

In addition to solid pay, job security for bus drivers is generally strong. Between 2018 and 2028, according to the Bureau of Labor Statistics, the field is expected to see a growth rate of 5 percent, which matches the average projections for other jobs in the United States. As the size of student bodies increases, the need for bus drivers will continue to expand, and there is a shortage of good candidates in many school districts. If you can keep up a clean driving record and you'll look forward to working with children every day, this could be a great fit for you.

CHAPTER 11

A DIFFERENT DESK IN SCHOOL

Remember the desk you sat at every day while you were in middle school? It was probably made of plastic or wood, with little cutouts for storing your school supplies. Though you sat at a desk like this every day, you probably never thought about the other desks that were in your school!

One of the most important positions for any educational institution is that of secretary. Much more than just the person who answers the phone or checks you out if you have to leave early, these talented professionals are given a lot of important responsibilities that they must take care of every day—in addition to completing unique projects from time to time. Though sitting behind the secretary's desk can be challenging and chaotic from time to time, most of these administrators love their job because they get to work around kids and help schools operate efficiently.

A COMPLEX JOB

If you want to find work as a school secretary, you must be able to combine two important qualities: good people skills and the ability to keep track of detailed information. The larger the school you work in, the busier the office will be. One of your biggest responsibilities is to help make the school run smoothly. You will have a great deal of contact with both students and various adults—from parents to teachers to administrators—and you will be asked to take care of important tasks every day.

School secretaries typically tie together all the loose ends that go with working in a school setting. The specific things you do over the course of an average day will vary based on whether you work in an elementary, middle, or high school, and the special projects you're asked to work on will always be varied. If you are in an elementary school, you might

School secretaries help keep track of attendance, school visitors, parent phone calls, and more.

find yourself working with vendors to set up a book fair in addition to your regular duties. In a middle school or high school, you might be asked to help organize a teen health fair or an after-school event.

Successful school secretaries are polite and pleasant—but firm and strong when necessary. They must be able to function well in an environment that will frequently be chaotic. They are well organized and calm in the face of crisis.

School secretaries must also respect the fact that they'll have access to some information that is strictly confidential. For example, a secretary will know which children are under the care of the Department of Social Services and which ones live in a shelter or a foster home. They'll also know which children are involved in custody disputes or are at the school under other special circumstances. They always protect the privacy of each student, regardless of their situation outside of the school.

As gatekeeper of the principal's office, a school secretary is the first person most parents and visitors will encounter when they enter the school. Secretaries may also meet with newcomers to the community who want to enroll their children; school supply salespeople; newspaper reporters in search of a story; and police officers looking for a particular student. They need to make

certain that each person is treated appropriately and with respect.

In addition, school secretaries sometimes encounter angry or upset parents who demand to see the principal or a specific teacher immediately.

Excellent typing skills aren't always a requirement to become a school secretary, but they certainly help.

They need to know how to react to these parents in a way that calms—rather than escalates—the situation. They also encounter adults, including parents without legal custody of their children, who want to have a child released from school but who aren't listed as an authorized guardian. In situations like these, school secretaries become part of the team effort that goes into assuring the safety of each child.

If you want a career working with children where you'll be respected for both your competence in managing detailed information and your ability to work well with all kinds of people, a position as a school secretary might be right for you.

GETTING BEHIND THE DESK

If you're interested in becoming a school secretary, the only thing you'll need is a high school diploma. However, computer skills and experience working in a hectic office setting are highly valued by all school districts. Some positions require that candidates be able to type a certain number of words per minute, as secretaries must do a lot of computer work. Taking business courses in high school or at a community college can also help you to land a job. Experience working with children, perhaps as a camp counselor or volunteer coach, is also highly valued.

The many skills that secretaries use on a daily basis are generally acquired through on-the-job training, which often continues for years. For example, if the school district introduces a new method of keeping track of standardized test scores, the school secretary may be sent to workshops to learn to use the software required to do the job. In addition, many school systems offer in-house courses on how to use popular software programs that are used every day.

The total compensation for most secretaries is very fair, especially considering that no advanced education is required to succeed in the position. Secretaries who work year-round (typically in high school positions) earn more than those who have the summers off, but nearly all secretaries will receive excellent benefits. In many school districts, unions represent secretaries and other administrative workers. These unions fight for regular pay raises, increased benefits, and many other quality-of-life improvements for their members.

CHAPTER 12

TEACHER'S . . . ASSISTANT?

Teachers—from kindergarten all the way to high school—take on one of the most important and challenging roles in society: educating young people. In modern times, with advanced technology, evolving standards, and governmental regulation, it can often be tough for instructors to get their jobs done. This is where teacher assistants (TAs) come in. Instead of conducting classes and coming up with tests for students, TAs instead focus on making it easier for the teacher to handle their tasks effectively. Daily responsibilities for a TA may include keeping attendance records, monitoring students on their lunch break, or even tutoring a child one-on-one. This is the perfect career for those who don't find college a good option but who still want to work with children in a school setting.

EMBRACING THE TA

Some of the most important characteristics required for an aspiring TA are patience and the ability to remain calm and even-tempered. As with most jobs that involve close contact with children, these skills will be invaluable. Because your daily duties may change from week to week, depending on the needs of the teacher or the class, you must be able to adapt quickly and confidently to new situations.

There are many different forms that a teacher assistant position can take. Some TA opportunities are offered part-time, and some are considered full-time. A part-time TA may only be expected to work for a few hours each day or only come in a few days of the week. A full-time TA, on the other hand, will be expected to work a schedule similar to a teacher's, and they're expected to complete a lot of daily, weekly, monthly, and yearly tasks.

In addition to classroom work, some TAs will be asked to work outside, supervising recesses or accompanying students on field trips. Depending on your specific assignments, your employer may require that you spend a lot of time on your feet.

There are many types of teacher assistants, depending on whether the job is within an elementary, middle, or high school. The responsibilities of the job also vary widely and can be based on a specific teacher's needs. In an elementary school setting, some TAs are hired for a specific task, such as supervising lunch sessions or playground time. Others are hired

Teacher assistants aren't available in every school district, but TAs can greatly improve the classroom experience for students. They're able to supervise group projects, give special attention to kids who need it, and lighten the load on the regular teacher.

to provide extra attention, working with children individually or in small groups under the direction of a classroom teacher.

In middle schools and high schools, teacher assistants are sometimes called teacher aides or instructional aides. In general, their responsibilities

are more specialized than those who work with younger children. For example, if you enjoy technology, you might want to search for a TA position for a high school's computer lab, helping students learn to use software and helping them find the information they need for their assignments.

Another major area of specialization for teacher assistants is in special education. The workers in these positions are sometimes called aides. The trend in education in the 21st century has been to place children with special needs in the regular classroom setting whenever possible. In many cases, this wouldn't be possible without a qualified aide. A child with a severe physical disability may be assigned an aide to help them with everything from getting in between classrooms to feeding and personal care. A child with severe behavioral problems may require an assistant to help them manage their aggression so that they can function in a regular classroom without disrupting classmates. Teacher assistants are also assigned to provide support for children for whom English is a second language and for children who simply need extra help or homework assistance.

A good TA can make a significant contribution to the well-being of one child or a group of children. It's often an assistant who spends the most time with a child who's having difficulty in a particular subject, especially if they're part of a large class. By working in a one-on-one or small group setting, the TA can help the teacher assess the difficulties and progress of struggling students. The teacher can use this information to come up with lessons that will make things easier for everyone in the class. An assistant who's involved with a group of children, perhaps working in a classroom or supervising a "time-out" room for kids who have misbehaved, contributes to the orderly atmosphere of a school, making it a better place for teachers to teach and children to learn.

GETTING IN THE CLASSROOM

To become a teacher assistant, you must have a high school education at minimum. Many school systems also require some college work, usually courses in child development, though it's rare that TAs need to have a college degree.

Many community colleges offer two-year associate's degree programs that can prepare you for a TA job. Some states require that teacher assistants pass a basic skills test before they begin work, while other states require full certification. No matter what level of preparation they bring to the position, TAs almost always receive on-the-job training. This will include instruction on software, policies, and procedures for each specific school and district.

The more training and education you have, the more likely you'll be to find a position as a classroom assistant that involves hands-on instruction, such as tutoring or reviewing homework. Nonteaching positions, such as those that primarily involve

If you have the knowledge to do so, as a TA you'll probably be asked to help students who are struggling in a teacher's class.

supervision outside the classroom (in the cafeteria, playground, parking lot, and so on) require less training and experience. Employers also look for prior experience working with children in all applicants. If you have held a position as a counselor at a summer camp, assisted at a day care center, or volunteered to help coach a youth team, be certain to mention this experience on your résumé or during an interview.

Once you have secured a position as a teacher assistant, opportunities to advance are typically dependent upon acquiring more education. Some school systems offer their employees tuition assistance to help them improve and expand their skills, and taking classes at a local college over the course of several years can help you earn a degree at an affordable price.

Teachers, in general, are getting harder to come by, with shortages all across the United States. For this reason, opportunities for teaching assistants are growing. The demand for TAs is greatest in areas experiencing an increase in population and school enrollments. Applicants who speak a second language, particularly Spanish, will catch the attention of a school district because bilingual staff members can better communicate with students and families whose primary language is not English. The number of TA positions centered on working alongside students with special needs is expected to increase, as the country continues to foster inclusive school programs for these children.

As with many occupations that require no advanced education, turnover among teacher assistants is high, creating a regular stream of job openings. According to the Bureau of Labor Statistics, from 2018 to 2028, positions in this field are expected to increase by 4 percent, which is close to the national average across all jobs. New opportunities for teacher assistants are also expected to develop as school districts establish after-school and summer programs for their students.

GLOSSARY

benefit A type of compensation for work not included in regular pay.

bookmobile A large van or truck stocked with books and other materials that travels to day care centers, schools, and youth clubs that don't have their own libraries.

certification Evidence of achievement of a particular level of expertise in a particular area.

child development The process through which a child acquires mental, physical, social, and emotional skills.

confidential Private.

custody The legal right to take care of a child.

direct services Work that involves ongoing contact with a person who is being taught or assisted.

enrichment activities Opportunities for children to learn new skills and concepts and explore their creativity in areas like dance, music, theater, and the visual arts.

enroll To officially join something.

entrepreneur Someone who opens their own business.

human services A professional field that involves helping people in need.

indirect services Work that involves arranging, evaluating, or otherwise providing a particular type of assistance needed by an individual.

in-service training Courses, workshops, or other forms of education provided by one's employer.

residential facility A place where people live who need the kind of assistance and support that can't be provided in their home.

résumé A document listing someone's work experience and professional qualifications.

salaried Describing a position in which a worker is paid a yearly rate instead of an hourly wage.

special education Programs designed to provide assistance to help children address physical, mental, emotional, and behavioral challenges that make it difficult for them to learn.

special needs Physical, mental, emotional, and social difficulties experienced by some children.

turnover The number of people who move through an industry.

versatility The ability to adjust one's performance or teaching approach to meet the needs of a particular individual or audience.

Association for Early Learning Leaders

1250 S. Capital of Texas Highway
Building 3, Suite 400
Austin, TX 78746
(800) 537-1118
Website: https://earlylearningleaders.org
Facebook: @EarlyLearningLeaders
Twitter: @AELLeaders

This nonprofit organization educates and trains the various professionals that interact and teach children. Connecting business owners, teachers, and caregivers to resources and conferences, this association aims to improve early childcare across the United States.

Child Welfare League of Canada (CWLC)

123 Slater Street, 6th floor
Ottawa, ON K1P 5H2
Canada
Website: http://www.cwlc.ca

The CWLC is a membership organization that promotes the safety and health of all children. The group's site offers information on programs and policies affecting Canada's most vulnerable young people.

Coaching Association of Canada

2451 Riverside Drive
Ottawa, ON K1H 7X7
Canada
(613) 235-5000
Website: http://www.coach.ca
Facebook: @coach.ca
Twitter: @CAC_ACE

This organization brings coaches together with teams that need leadership. It offers training and other resources for new coaches and those who want to improve.

Council for Professional Recognition
2460 16th Street NW
Washington, DC 20009-3547
(800) 424-4310
Website: http://cdacouncil.org
Facebook, Instagram, and Twitter: @cdacouncil
This organization's primary goal is to connect educators, caregivers, and anyone else who works with children to the education, training, and skills they need to do a good job. It offers a training program to help childcare workers earn the Child Development Associate (CDA) credential.

National Association for the Education of Young Children (NAEYC)
1313 L Street NW, Suite 500
Washington, DC 20005-4101
(202) 232-8777
Website: http://www.naeyc.org
Facebook, Instagram, and Twitter: @NAEYC
Dedicated to improving the lives of children in early education, NAEYC is an influential organization for early childhood educators. Its website includes a catalog of early childhood resource materials.

National Child Care Association (NCCA)
P.O. Box 2948
Merrifield, VA
(877) 537-6222
Website: http://www.nccanet.org

This membership organization provides networking and professional development opportunities for people involved in childhood care and education.

National Education Association (NEA)

1201 16th Street NW
Washington, DC 20036-3290
(202) 833-4000
Website: https://nea.org
Facebook, Instagram, and Twitter: @NEAToday
The largest teacher's union in the United States, the NEA offers details on how to become a teacher, articles on current events, and more information for anyone who's interested in getting into education.

FOR FURTHER READING

American Academy of Pediatrics. *BLAST: Babysitter Lessons and Safety Training.* Burlington, MA: Jones & Bartlett Learning, 2016.

Ardely, Anthony. *I Can Be a Librarian.* New York, NY: Gareth Stevens Publishing, 2019.

Cope, Ed, and Mark Partington. *Sports Coaching: A Theoretical and Practical Guide.* New York, NY: Routledge, 2019.

Freedman, Jeri. *Careers in Child Care.* New York, NY: Rosen Publishing, 2015.

Given-Wilson, Rachel, and Annalise Silivanch. *Your Future as a Teacher.* New York, NY: Rosen YA, 2020.

Pawlewski, Sarah. *Careers: The Graphic Guide to Finding the Perfect Job for You.* New York, NY: DK Publishing, 2015.

Rissman, Rebecca, and Melissa Higgins. *Babysitter's Backpack: Everything You Need to Be a Safe, Smart, and Skilled Babysitter.* North Mankato, MN: Capstone Young Readers, 2015.

Sunseri, Sophia Natasha. *Working as a Teacher in Your Community.* New York, NY: Rosen Publishing, 2016.

ABOUT THE AUTHOR

Morgan Williams lives in New York with her husband and two corgis, Tate and Isabelle. She enjoys traveling the world to take in different cultures and cuisines. She's gone on adventures in Japan, Peru, and Iran.

CREDITS

Cover (icon background) HelenField/Shutterstock.com; cover (main image), pp. 14, 48 Monkey Business Images/Shutterstock.com; p. 7 NicolasMcComber/Getty Images; p. 9 skynesher/Getty Images; p. 17 Jamie Garbutt/Getty Images; p. 22 Jose Luis Pelaez Inc/Getty Images; p. 25 Oksana Kuzmina/Shutterstock.com; p. 29 JGI/Jamie Grill/Getty Images; p. 32 Westend61/Getty Images; pp. 36, 91 Photographee.eu/Shutterstock.com; p. 39 Rawpixel.com/Shutterstock.com; p. 42 Rido/Shutterstock.com; p. 44 Epics/Getty Images; p. 51 AlohaHawaii/Shutterstock.com; p. 53 goodluz/Shutterstock.com; p. 57 New Africa/Shutterstock.com; p. 59 Africa Studio/Shutterstock.com; p. 64 ESB Professional/Shutterstock.com; p. 66 RossHelen/Shutterstock.com; p. 68 Flamingo Images/Shutterstock.com; p. 73 sirtravelalot/Shutterstock.com; p. 76 Kzenon/Shutterstock.com; p. 81 Silvrshootr/Getty Images; p. 83 Antonio Guillem/Shutterstock.com; p. 88 stockfour/Shutterstock.com.

Designer: Brian Garvey; Editor: Siyavush Saidian